SPACE STATION ACADEMY

DESTINATION:
URANUS

SALLY SPRAY AND
MARK RUFFLE

WAYLAND

First published in Great Britain in 2023
by Wayland
© Hodder and Stoughton Limited, 2023

HB ISBN: 978 1 5263 2092 6
PB ISBN: 978 1 5263 2093 3

Editor: Paul Rockett
Design and illustration: Mark Ruffle
www.rufflebrothers.com

MIX
Paper from
responsible sources
FSC® C104740
FSC
www.fsc.org

Printed in Dubai

Wayland
An imprint of Hachette Children's Group
Part of Hodder & Stoughton
Carmelite House
50 Victoria Embankment
London EC4Y 0DZ

An Hachette UK company
www.hachette.co.uk
www.hachettechildrens.co.uk

Picture credits:
Page 30 NASA/JPL; page 31 NASA/JPL, NASA/JPL/USGS

SAFETY PRECAUTIONS

We recommend adult supervision at all times while doing the experiments in this book. Always be aware that ingredients may contain allergens, so check the packaging for allergens if there is a risk of an allergic reaction. Anyone with a known allergy must avoid these.

- Wear an apron and cover surfaces.
- Tie back long hair.
- Ask an adult for help with cutting.
- Check all ingredients for allergens.
- Clear up all spills straight away.

Contents

Meet the team

Dr Bott

Mo

Stella

Max

Xing

Melody

Welcome to Space Station Academy, the amazing interstellar school that travels through space. Come on board and learn about our solar system.

Left step, right step, front step, side step. Reach up left! Now to the right! Stretch out, kids – as far as you can!

I love being in gym class!

It's early morning and the Space Academy is nearing Uranus. Meanwhile, the students are busy exercising in the gym.

5

A while later the students and Dr Bott head off in the space pod ...

Tell us about Uranus, Dr Bott.

Uranus is the seventh planet out from the Sun. It's not the furthest planet in the solar system, but it is the coldest, with an average temperature of -195°C.

And because it's so far out, it takes a long time to orbit the Sun. One orbit takes 84 Earth years.

And, it's enormous!

It has a diameter of 50,724 km, it's one of two outer planets that are called ice giants.

A day on Uranus is 17 Earth hours.

Watch Uranus closely and tell me what you notice ...

It's spinning on its side!

That's right! It got knocked off its axis, perhaps in a collison with another planet millions of years ago. When Uranus tipped over, its moons went with it, still orbiting around the middle, which is now top to bottom! Let's go and visit some of the largest moons ...

Scientists have found 27 moons around Uranus, but there could be many more.

This is Oberon. Its surface is dark and full of craters and there's a tall mountain over 6 km high.

There is very little gravity here.

Oberon

Low gravity means things weigh less!

I can get this right over my head.

We can lift these stones easily! I love this moon gym!

Would you like to try, Dr Bott? We should try to stay fit in space.

Miranda

Gulp!

Wheeee!

You should try this!

Okay, you fitness fanatics, welcome to the moon Miranda.

We're on the icy edge of Verona Rupes, the 20-km-high, tallest cliff in the solar system.

I can float down!

You're going to parachute down. It'll take 10 minutes to reach the ground!

Miranda's diameter is only 472 km, making this enormous cliff even more remarkable and spectacular.

Steering the parachute would keep you fit, Dr Bott!

There's Uranus! How far away is it?

From here it's almost 130,000 km away. Can you see the rings? It has 13 rings in all, they differ in colour from grey to red to blue.

Let's go and take a closer look.

I don't need to be fit!

Miranda orbits Uranus every 1.4 days. It moves quicker than we are!

15

We can see the rings more clearly from here. They are made up of icy rocks and boulders. The ice in the rings is quite dark and not reflective, making the rings hard to see.

The ring system also contain 13 small inner moons, orbiting Uranus in complicated paths that overlap. Some of these moons may collide in the distant future when their orbits cross.

We think the outer ring is made of dust and debris coming off the moon named Mab.

The brightest ring is called Epsilon. This ring is kept in place by two shepherd moons, called Cordelia and Ophelia, which orbit either side of the ring.

We could be your shepherd moons.

We could all go running together!

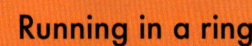

Running in a ring!

Keep you fit and healthy like us!

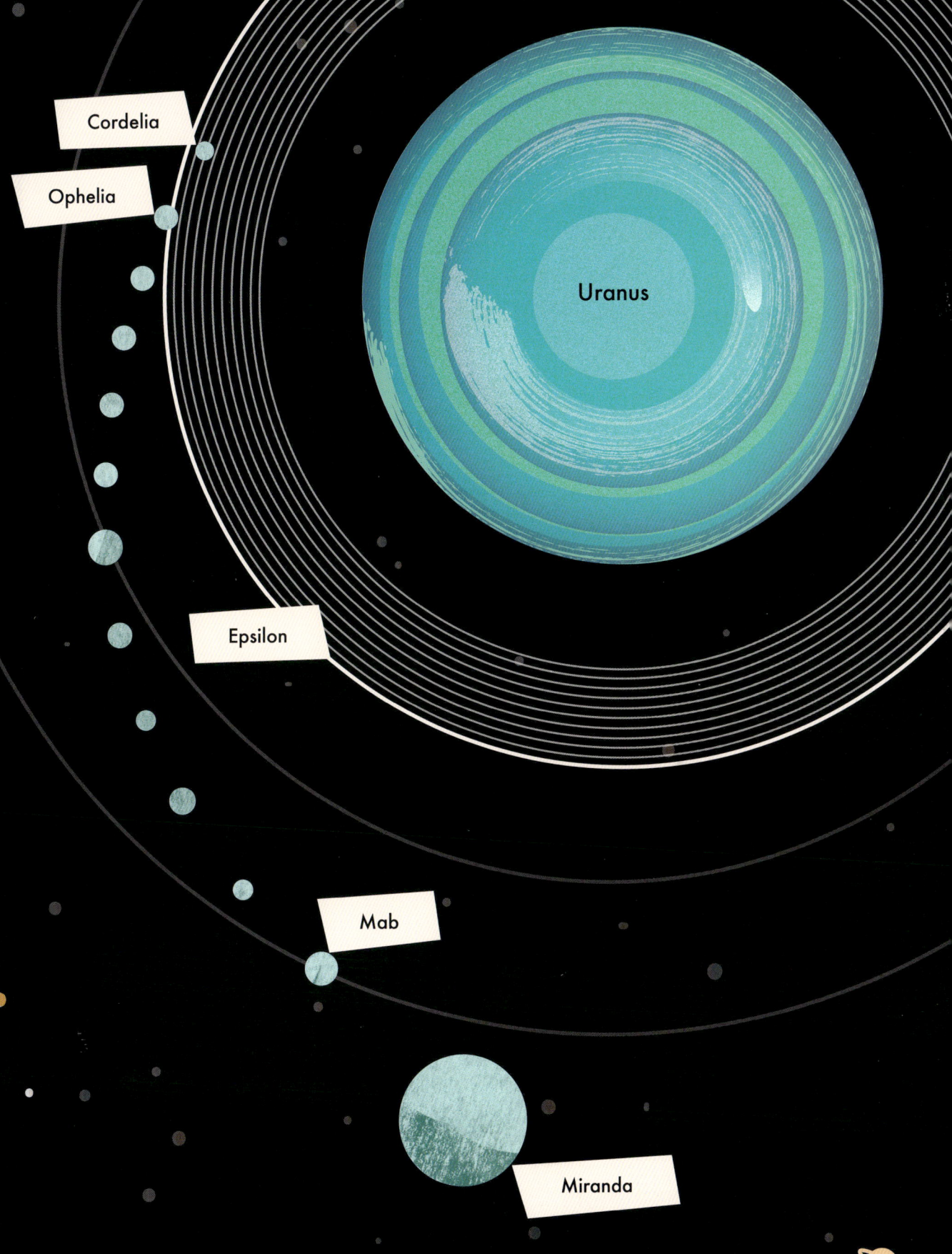

Cordelia

Ophelia

Uranus

Epsilon

Mab

Miranda

Once safely back inside the Space Academy, the students set to work …

Space Station Activities

The Space Academy gang have been so inspired by their mission to Uranus, they wanted to find out more. Will you join them?

Dr Bott's Space Experiment

Use these recipes to make your own slime – like the slushy, slimy layer on Uranus. Try them out and see which one works best! It's important that you have an adult with you to supervise.

Glue slime
• 100 ml PVA white glue
• ½ tsp bicarbonate of soda
• Gel food colouring or poster paint
• 1 tsp saline solution
• Glitter (optional)

Method
Squeeze glue into a bowl.
Mix in the bicarbonate of soda.
Add a few drops of food colour or paint. Mix again.
Add the saline solution and mix again, until the slime starts to form and come away from the sides of the bowl.
Add glitter and mix together with your hands.

Try this recipe with a squirt of shaving foam and see what happens! Try a marble effect with the colours!

Store your slime in an air-tight container in the fridge.

Experiment Variations
What happens if you leave your slime out of the fridge? Is it better kept in a fridge? Try the recipes with different soaps or washing up liquid – do you get the same slimy results?

Melody's Uranus Fact

The moons of Uranus are named after characters from plays written by William Shakespeare, apart from two, Ariel and Umbriel, which came from a poem written by Alexander Pope (Ariel is also a character in Shakespeare's *The Tempest*).

Max's Extra Uranus Fact:

Uranus is one of only two planets that rotates east to west. The other planet that does this is Venus. So, on Uranus (and Venus) sunrise happens in the west and sunset in the east.

Xing's Uranus Maths Problem

These are the five major moons of Uranus and their sizes in km.

Which is the largest moon? Which is the smallest moon? What is the sum of their diameters? What's the average diameter of these moons?

Oberon
1,523 km

Titania
1,578 km

Umbriel
1,169 km

Ariel
1,158 km

Miranda
472 km

Answer: Titania, Miranda, 5,900 km, 1,180 km

Stella's Uranus Picture Gallery

Uranus looks very still and pale in this image.

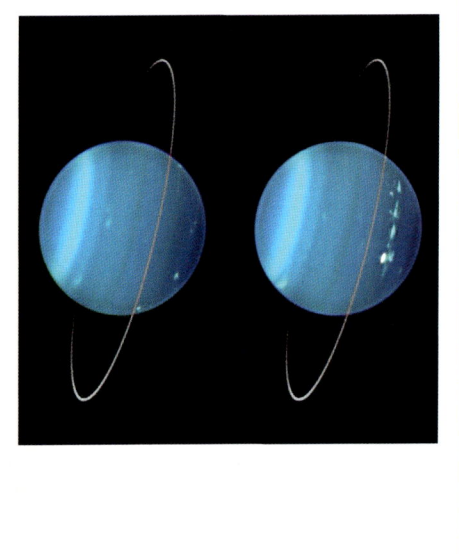

These images show both sides of Uranus and its rings.

Mo's Research Project

Can you find out more about the rings of Uranus? How old are they? How big? Could you make a map showing each ring and the moons that orbit within the rings?

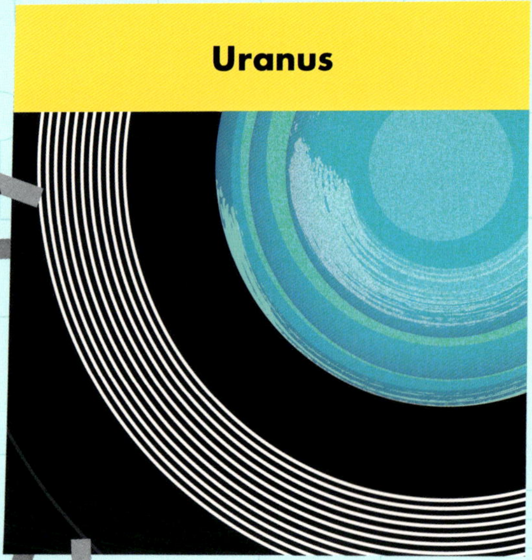

Uranus

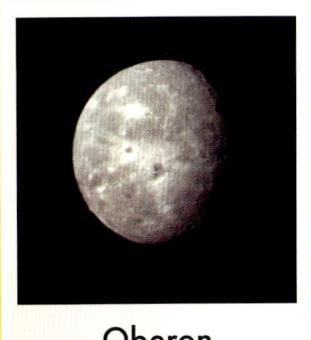
Oberon

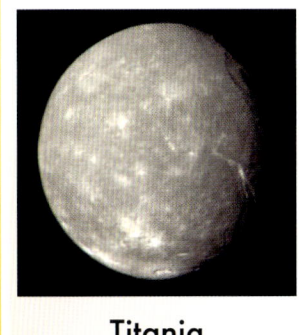
Titania

Umbriel

These are the five major moons. Take a look at the different textures. How do you think the surface marks got there?

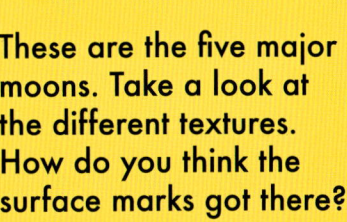
Ariel

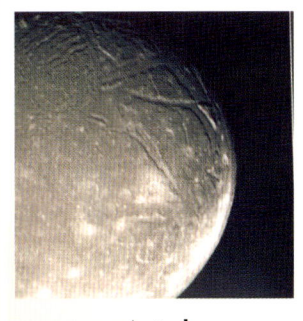
Miranda

Further information

Wonderful websites
spaceplace.nasa.gov/all-about-uranus/en/
kids.kiddle.co/Uranus
www.planetsforkids.org/planet-uranus.html
www.ducksters.com/science/uranus.php
solarsystem.nasa.gov/moons/uranus-moons/overview

Brilliant books
Dr Maggie's Grand Tour of the Solar System by Dr Maggie Aderin-Pocock (Buster Books, 2019)
So Many Questions About Space by Sally Spray (Wayland, 2022)
Wonders of the Night Sky by Professor Raman Prinja (Wayland, 2022)

Glossary

atmosphere – the layer of gas surrounding a planet
axis – the imaginary line around which an object, such as a planet, rotates
core – the centre of something, such as a planet
crater – a large, bowl-shaped hole in the surface of something, such as a moon
diameter – the measurement across the middle of a sphere or circle
gravity – the force of attraction that pulls one thing towards another
holographic – describes a hologram, a 3-D image that looks solid, not flat
interstellar – describes something that is located or happens between stars
mantle – the layer of a planet that surrounds its core
moon – a natural body that orbits a planet
orbit – to travel around a star or planet or the path taken around a star or planet
reflective – describes something, such as a shiny surface, that reflects light
scientist – a person who researches, tests and learns about the natural world
solar system – the Sun and the objects in orbit around it
valley – a dip in the land, usually surrounded by hills or mountains

Index